The English texts of the following songs are printed by permission of
Reuter and Reuter Förlags AB: *Cradle Song, Cinderella, Trolls' Lullaby,
Johnny's Song, Dragonfly, Beyond the Twilight, Josephina Blues.*

Editorial work and lay–out by Ulf Goran Åhslund and Sid Jansson

English translation by Paul Britten Austin

Music origination by Olle Karlsson

Illustrations by Sid Jansson

Printed in Great Britain

C000198243

Play Guitar

by Ulf Goran

FOREWORD

If you have never plucked a note of music on the guitar in your life, this
tutor has been specially designed for you. And even if you have, and can
play quite a bit, it's still for you! In a clear and simple way it gives you all
the basic information you need on how to accompany and how to play
tunes on the guitar.

The accompaniments emphasize the special character of each melody,
using counter-melodies as well as traditional chords. The mixture of
'arrangements' and 'accompaniments' in this tutor can lead you on to a
classical fingering technique, if your tastes lie in that direction; and it also
shows what a many-sided and really expressive instrument the guitar is.

The tablature (see page 9) used in this book has proved itself a good
practical introduction to everyday playing, but ordinary music notation
is also thoroughly explained. Here the 'Note-Finder', first found on page
25, with its combination of five-line notation and tablature is invaluable.
A further development of the Note-Finder is the 'Spinner', which is explained in Book 2. This helps you translate the five-line notation into
tablature.

Good Playing!

CONTENTS

STRING NUMBERS

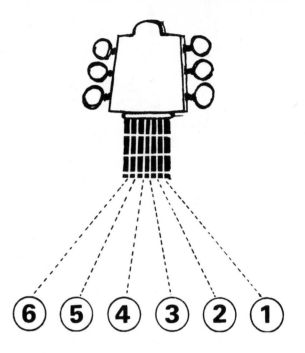

On the inside cover pages: Parts of the Guitar, Here is how you tune your Guitar,
What you should demand of your Guitar, How to look after your Guitar,
How you change strings, and a Gramophone record.

GREENSLEEVES ✳

Accompaniment on open strings

The melody line begins on the same note as String ①

After you've checked up on the strings' numbers on the previous page you'll be able to play the tune. The numbers above the words tell you when to pluck. Listen to the record too.

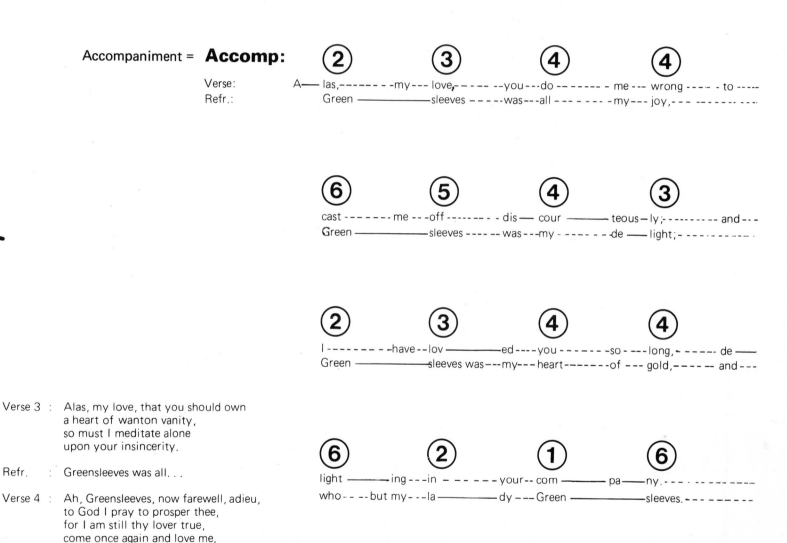

Accompaniment = **Accomp:**

	②	③	④	④
Verse:	A— las,------ -my--- love,----- -you---do ------- - me --- wrong ---- - to -----
Refr.:	Green ————sleeves ----- was---all --- - - --- my--- joy,--- -------

	⑥	⑤	④	③
cast ------- me ---off ------- - dis— cour ————teous—ly;--------- and ---
Green ————sleeves ----- - was---my ------ - -de — light;-----------

	②	③	④	④
I ------- --have --lov ————ed ----you ------ -so ----long,------ de ——
Green ————sleeves was---my--- heart------- -of --- gold,----- and ---

	⑥	②	①	⑥
light ————ing---in ----- ----your-- com ————pa—ny.---- - - -----
who-- --but my---la————dy ---Green ————sleeves.---- -----

Verse 1 : Alas, my love, you do me wrong
to cast me off discourteously;
and I have loved you so long,
delighting in your company.

Refr. : Greensleeves was all my joy,
Greensleeves was my delight;
Greensleeves was my heart of gold,
and who but my lady Greensleeves.

Verse 2 : If you intend thus to disdain,
it does the more enrapture me,
and even so, I still remain
a lover in captivity.

Refr. : Greensleeves was all. . .

Verse 3 : Alas, my love, that you should own
a heart of wanton vanity,
so must I meditate alone
upon your insincerity.

Refr. : Greensleeves was all. . .

Verse 4 : Ah, Greensleeves, now farewell, adieu,
to God I pray to prosper thee,
for I am still thy lover true,
come once again and love me.

Refr. : Greensleeves was all. . .

16th-century English melody

All melodies have been recorded on a 33 rpm disc, which you will find at the back of the tutor.

WHAT SHALL WE DO ✳6
Accompaniment 1

The melody line begins on the same note as String ② (See string numbers p. 2).

Accomp ⑥   ⑥   ⑥   ⑥

Verse: What- - - - shall--we---do - - - - - —with--the-- drunk——— en - - - - - - - sail——— or?- - - - - -
Refr.: Hoo——————— ray - - - - - - - - - and--up - - - - - - she - - - - - - ris——— es,- - - -

④   ④   ④   ④

What- - - - -shall--we---do - - - - - with--the-- drunk—— en - - - - - sail——— or?- - - - - - -
Hoo——————— ray - - - - - - - - and--up - - - - - - she - - - - ris——— es, - - - - -

⑥   ⑥   ⑥   ⑥

What- - - - -shall--we-- do- - - - - - with--the-- drunk—— en - - - - - - sail——— or - - - - - -
Hoo——————— ray - - - - - - - and--up - - - - -she - - - - - -ris——— es - - - - - -

④   ⑤   ⑥   ⑥

ear———ly - - - - - in - - - - the - - - - -morn——————— ing? - - - - - - - -
ear———ly - - - - - in - - - - the - - - - morn——————— ing. - - - - - -

Shanty from the British Isles, to an Irish dance tune

Listen to the record and learn the *word and melody rhythm* by joining in. At the same time follow the words, at the side here, and clap your hands at each string number. This will give you the *accompaniment rhythm*. Compare with the guitar on the record.
Finally, accompany on your guitar with the same rhythm as you've been clapping.
Notice that each string number lies immediately above the syllable in the words at which you must pluck the string.
Notice, too, how numbers and text are *always divided up* in such a way that you can *see* the rhythm.
What you *see* agrees with what you *hear*.

This method is applied throughout this tutor.

American folk-tune

SHE'LL BE COMIN' ROUND THE MOUNTAIN
Accompaniment

The melody line begins on the same note as string ⑤

Accomp: ④   ④   ④   ④

Verse 1: She'll--be---- com — in'--- round the --- moun-tain--- when--she--- comes,----- (when---she--- comes) ---- --She'll-be-----

Verse 2: She'll--be---- driv — in'---- six --- white-hors — es ---- when--she--- comes,----- (when--she--- comes) -----She'll-be-----

Verse 3: Oh,----we'll---all ----go--- out --- to -- -meet--her --- when--she--- comes,----- (when·-she--- comes) ------- Oh,----we'll---

    ④   ④   ⑤   ⑤

com —in'---- round--the---- moun-tain---- when--she----- comes,----- (when--she--- comes)------She'll-be-----

driv — in'----six ----white·hors — es --- when--she--- comes,------ (when--she---- comes) -----She'll-be-----

all----go--- out ---to ---meet -- her --- when--she -- comes,---- (when---she--- comes) ----- We--- will---

    ④   ④   ③   ③

steam—in'---- and--- a ---- puf — fin',--Oh--- Lawd,-She -- won't--stop---for--- noth—in'; --- She'll--be----

driv — in'----six ----white--hors—es,--- She'll-be-----driv — in'---- six---- white--hors--es,-----She'll-be----

kill--- the ---old---red---roos--ter,----We --- will---kill---the ---old--- red ---roos--ter,--- And-- we'll--

    ④   ⑤   ④   ④

com—in'----round the ---moun-tain--- when--she--- comes.----- (when--she----comes)-------

driv—in'---- six ---white--hors—es ---- when--she--- comes.----- (when--she--comes)----- -

all ----have-- chick—en----- dump-lins ----when--she----comes. ---- (when--she--comes)----

WHAT SHALL WE DO
Accompaniment 2

RIGHT HAND

The melody line begins on String ②

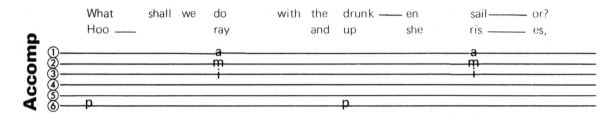

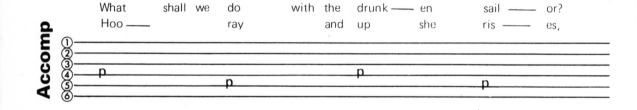

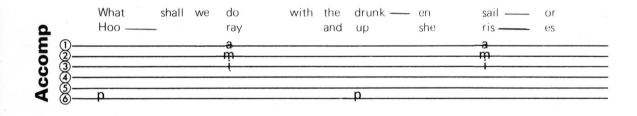

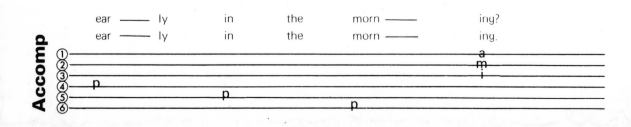

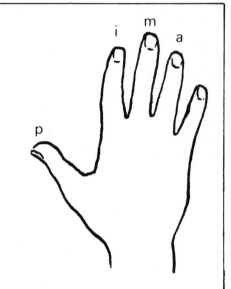

The fingers of the right hand are indicated by the internationally accepted *p, i, m, a* which are the first letters of each finger's Latin name.

On this page you'll find these right-hand letters written on long guitar-strings to show you how bit by bit you'll play with your right hand on the *open* strings.

Verse 1 : What shall we do with the drunken sailor, (3x) early in the morning?

Refr. : Hooray and up she rises, (3x) early in the morning.

Verse 2 : Put him in a long-boat until he's sober, (3x) early in the morning. (Refr.)

Verse 3 : Pull out the plug and wet him all over, (3x) early in the morning. (Refr.)

Verse 4 : Put him in the scuppers with a hose-pipe on him, (3x) early in the morning. (Refr.)

American Gospel

OH SINNERMAN *
Accompaniment 1

POSITION OF RIGHT HAND

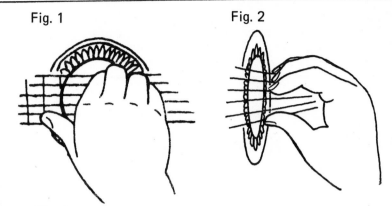

Fig. 1
The hand and fingers are at a right angles to the strings.

Fig. 2
The wrist is kept well away from the sound board.

The melody line begins on String ②

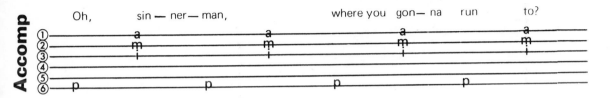

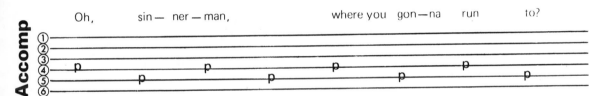

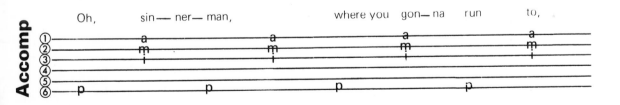

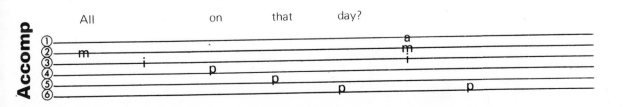

Verse 1: Oh, sinnerman, where you gonna run to, (3x)
All on that day?

Verse 2: Run to the rock, the rock was a-melting, (3x)
All on that day.

Verse 3: Run to the sea, the sea was a-boiling, (3x)
All on that day.

Verse 4: Run to the moon, the moon was a-bleeding, (3x)
All on that day.

Verse 5: Run to the Lord, Lord won't you hide me, (3x)
All on that day?

Verse 6: Run to the Devil, Devil was a-waiting, (3x)
All on that day.

Verse 7: Oh sinnerman, you oughta be a-praying, (3x)
All on that day.

DIAGRAM

Diagram = picture of strings and frets of neck.
Black dots = show where you must press down strings.
Rings = open strings belonging to the chord.
Figures in diagram = left-hand fingering.
Letters under diagram = right-hand fingering.

LEFT HAND ✳

The *left-hand fingers* are indicated by internationally accepted figures (see below).

RIGHT HAND

The thumb passes slowly over all strings *(arpeggio)* *from* string ⑥ *to* string ①
(See the arrowhead)

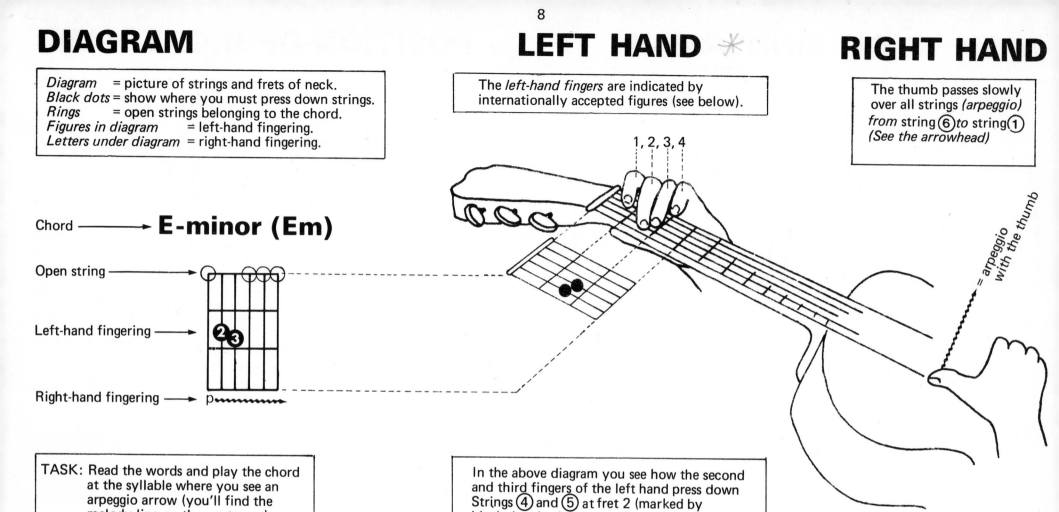

1, 2, 3, 4

Chord ——➤ **E-minor (Em)**

Open string

Left-hand fingering

Right-hand fingering ——➤ p〰〰〰

= arpeggio with the thumb

TASK: Read the words and play the chord at the syllable where you see an arpeggio arrow (you'll find the melody line on the next page).

In the above diagram you see how the second and third fingers of the left hand press down Strings ④ and ⑤ at fret 2 (marked by black dots in the diagram).

CRADLE SONG

Accompaniment

Words by Ulf Goran Åhslund

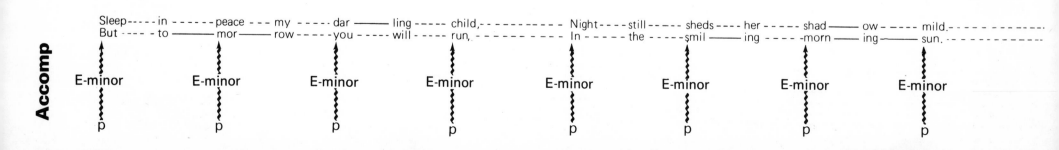

Sleep ----- in ----- peace --- my ----- dar —— ling ----- child, ----------- Night ---- still ----- sheds ---- her ----- shad —— ow ----- mild. ----------
But ----- to ----- mor ----- row ----- you ----- will ----- run, ----------- In ----- the ----- smil —— ing ---- -morn —— ing —— sun. ----

Accomp

E-minor   E-minor   E-minor   E-minor   E-minor   E-minor   E-minor   E-minor

p   p   p   p   p   p   p   p

TABLATURE

Throughout the 16th, 17th and 18th centuries tablature was the commonest system of notation for all stringed instruments of the plucked type (lute, vihuela and guitar). There are four main types of tablature: German, French, Italian and Spanish. The Spanish type, on which this tutor is based, was designed in the 16th century by the Spanish composer and vihuela-player Luys Milan.

Since tablature is a kind of shorthand, showing which frets to press, it has great advantages as an easy introduction to guitar-playing for anyone who cannot "read music". This is particularly true of the Spanish type, in which a number always tells you exactly where the note lies on the frets. But the one system — tablature — doesn't exclude the other — ordinary five-line musical notation. Each has its definite advantages, and they may well be used alongside the other.

A good example of a mixture of the two ways of writing out music is John Dowland's (1562–1626) famous "Seven Tears", in which he uses tablature for the lute but the usual notation for the other instruments in his ensemble.

Ordinary musical notation can be translated into tablature, or vice versa, by using the "Note-finder" (see p. 26) or the Note-finder Spinner in "Play Guitar, Book 2".

Fret numbers

The fret numbers are written out on tablature lines (symbolizing the six guitar strings). The fret numbers tell you which fret you must press the string down on (an open, unpressed string is indicated with an 0).

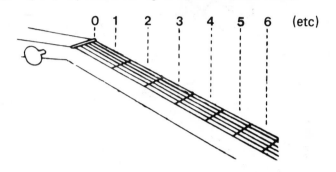

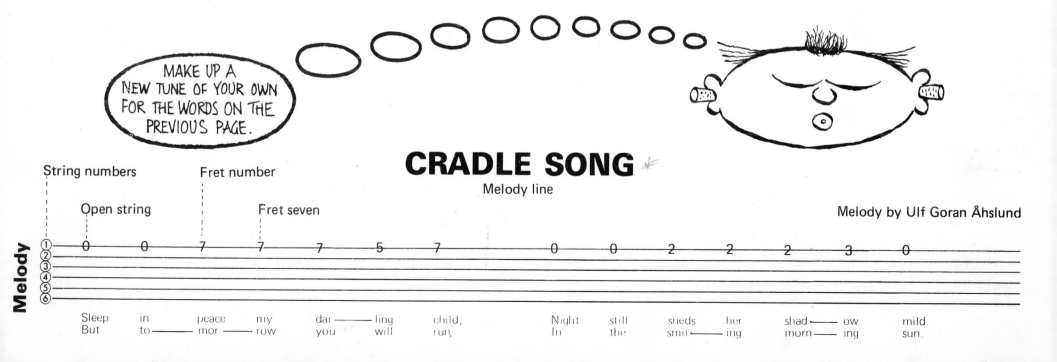

CRADLE SONG
Melody line

Melody by Ulf Goran Åhslund

Sleep in peace my dar—ling child, Night still sheds her shad—ow mild.
But to—mor—row you will run, In the smil—ing morn—ing sun.

POSITION OF LEFT HAND

As you see in the drawing, the neck of the guitar must not be allowed to slip down into the angle of the thumb.

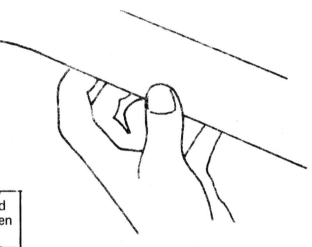

Beneath, you can distinguish between long and short notes by comparing the distances between the fret numbers. See also method on p. 4.

CINDERELLA

Melody line *Major* and *Minor*

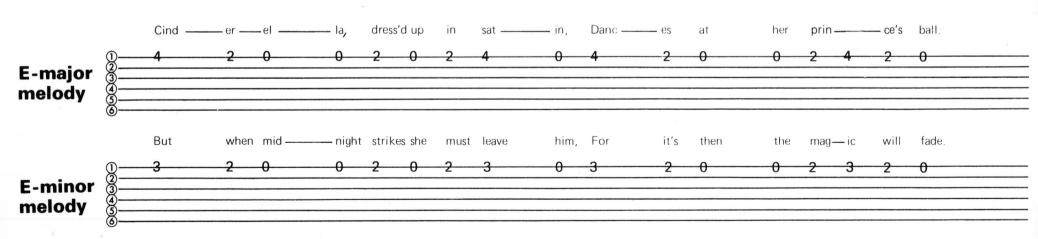

Fragment of an old French folk-song. Minor theme by Ulf Goran Åhslund

LEFT AND RIGHT HAND

CINDERELLA
Accompaniment

E-major = E

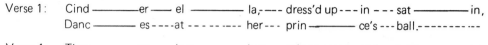
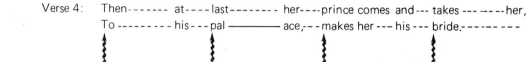

Verse 1: Cind ————er — el ———— la,--- dress'd up ---in --- sat ————in,
Danc ———— es ---at --------- her--- prin ———ce's--- ball.---------

Verse 4: Then------- at----last------- her----prince comes and--- takes ------her,
To --------- his-- pal ———— ace,-- makes her --- his --- bride.-----------

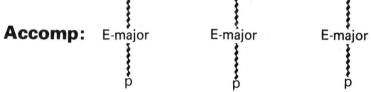

Accomp: E-major   E-major   E-major   E-major

p   p   p   p

MAJOR (Verse 1 & 4)
MINOR (Verse 2 & 3)

E-minor = Em

Verse 2: But---------when--mid ———— night--strikes she---- must--leave ------him,
For------- it's--- then ------- the--- mag —ic ---- will--- fade.- ------- -

Just--------- a----- shoe -------- they'll find--- on ---- the--- stair ———— case,
Search------- and---seek ------- her-- out--- ev' — ry ——where.- -------

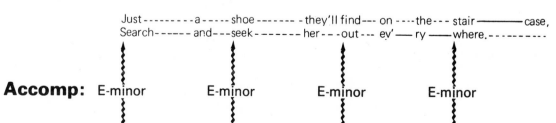

Accomp: E-minor   E-minor   E-minor   E-minor

p   p   p   p

Words by Ulf Goran Åhslund

NOTE VALUES

PAUSES

> Here you *read* and *tap out* the rhythms simultaneously.
> Figure or letter *not* in brackets = *read* and tap.
> Figure or letter *in* brackets = read but *don't tap*.

Semibreve 	𝅝					▬	= whole note pause
(whole note)	Count:	one	(two)	(three)	(four)		
Minim	𝅗𝅥		𝅗𝅥			▬	= half note pause
(half notes)	Count:	one	(two)	three	(four)		
Crotchet	𝅘𝅥	𝅘𝅥	𝅘𝅥	𝅘𝅥		𝄽	= quarter note pause
(quarter notes)	Count:	one	two	three	four		
Quaver	𝅘𝅥𝅮 𝅘𝅥𝅮	𝅘𝅥𝅮𝅘𝅥𝅮	𝅘𝅥𝅮𝅘𝅥𝅮𝅘𝅥𝅮𝅘𝅥𝅮			𝄾	= eight note pause
(eighth notes)	Count:	one &	two &	three &	four &		

DOTTED NOTE

A dot extends the length of the note by half again.
Which means that a half note (which is equal to two quarter notes) when dotted is equal to three quarter notes (See example below).

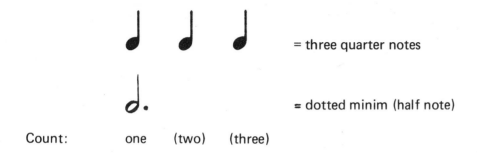

= three quarter notes

= dotted minim (half note)

Count: one (two) (three)

SOME RHYTHMIC EXAMPLES

Tap out the notes with a regular count.

Have a nice time!

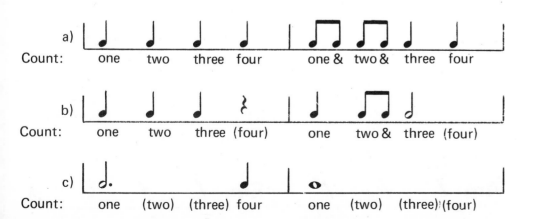

a)
Count: one two three four one & two & three four

b)
Count: one two three (four) one two & three (four)

c)
Count: one (two) (three) four one (two) (three) (four)

SOME RHYTHM INSTRUMENTS FOR THE FAMILY GROUP

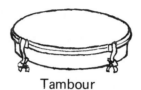

Tambour

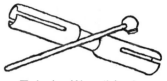

Tubular Woodblock
(double note)

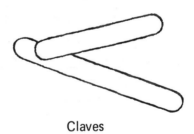

Claves

Triangle

Small Cymbals

Boxes
(e.g. matchboxes) covered with sandpaper

LEFT AND RIGHT HAND

Em

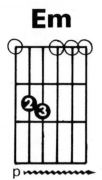

Am

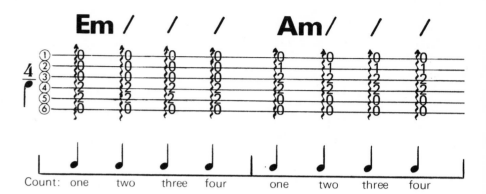

Count: one   two   three   four   one   two   three   four

This example is in
four-four time or
"four-in-a-bar".

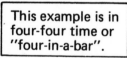

$\frac{4}{4}$ = C = four crotchets

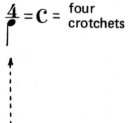

Time
signature

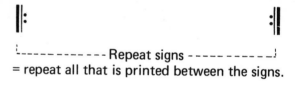

Repeat signs
= repeat all that is printed between the signs.

Bar   Down beat   Bar line   Repeat sign

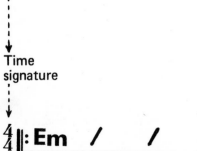

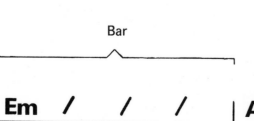

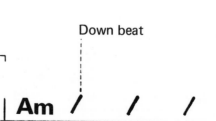

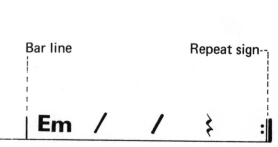

JOSHUA FOUGHT THE BATTLE OF JERICHO

Accompaniment

Negro Spiritual

This tune goes in 4/4 time.

The melody line begins on String ①

Same as preceding bar

Accomp : Em / / / | % | Am / / / | Em / / / :

Joshua ----- fought -- the bat ---- tle -- of ---------- Jer ------ i ------ cho, ------------------- Jer ------ i ------ cho, -------------- Jer ----- i ------ cho, ------
Joshua ---- fought -- the bat ---- tle -- of ---------- Jer ------ i ------ cho, ---- And ---- the --- walls ---- came --- a -- tum --- bl-ing -------- down. -------------- You --- may --

Accomp Em / / / | % | % | %

talk ----- a-bout --- your-kings ------ of ---------- Gid ------ e ------ on, ----- You ---- may --- talk ---- a --bout -- your -- man --- of --------- Saul, ------------------ But --- there's

Accomp Em / / / | % | Em ♪ Am ♪ | Em (Am) Em ♪

none ------ like ------ good ----- old ---- Josh ----- u ------ a ------ at ----- the --- bat --- tle -- of ------- Jer ----- i ------ cho. --------------------------

Refr. Joshua fought the battle of Jericho,
Jericho, Jericho,
Joshua fought the battle of Jericho,
And the walls came a tumbling down.

Verse 1: You may talk about your kings of Gideon,
You may talk about your man of Saul,
But there's none like good old Joshua
at the battle of Jericho. (Refr.)

Verse 2: Up to the walls of Jericho
He marched with spear in hand,
"Go blow those ram-horns," Joshua cried,
"Cause the battle is in my hands." (Refr.)

Verse 3: Then the lamb ram sheephorns began to blow,
The trumpets began to sound.
Joshua commanded the children to shout,
And the walls came a tumbling down. (Refr.)

Verse 4: There's no man like Joshua,
No man like Saul,
No man like Joshua
At the battle of Jericho. (Refr.)

CAPOTASTO

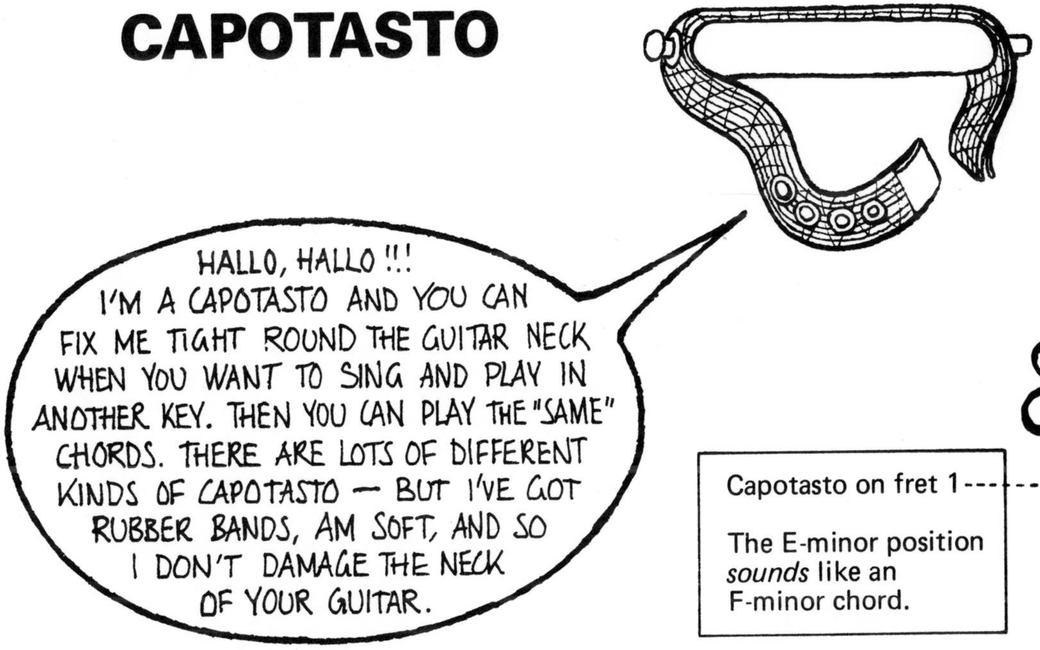

HALLO, HALLO !!!
I'M A CAPOTASTO AND YOU CAN FIX ME TIGHT ROUND THE GUITAR NECK WHEN YOU WANT TO SING AND PLAY IN ANOTHER KEY. THEN YOU CAN PLAY THE "SAME" CHORDS. THERE ARE LOTS OF DIFFERENT KINDS OF CAPOTASTO — BUT I'VE GOT RUBBER BANDS, AM SOFT, AND SO I DON'T DAMAGE THE NECK OF YOUR GUITAR.

Capotasto on fret 1 ---

The E-minor position *sounds* like an F-minor chord.

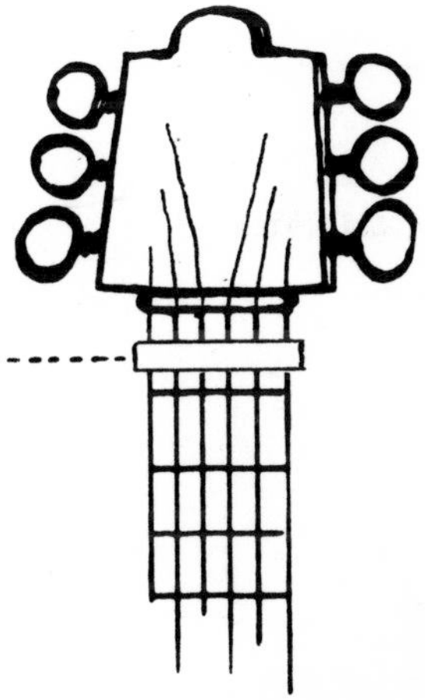

SORE FINGERTIPS

After playing the guitar for a while it's all too common for one's fingertips to become a trifle sore. But don't worry! After a week or so, when the skin on them has had time to grow thicker, the soreness will go away. Another point to bear in mind is that nylon strings are gentler on your fingertips and, together with a correct distance between the strings and frets (about 1 millimetre at fret 1), make for easier playing.

Other aches or pains

Other aches and pains while playing can be due to adopting a wrong sitting posture, to getting all tensed up, or to playing too long at a time, without brief intervals of relaxation.

The proper way to sit

Sit on a chair — not an armchair — of the right height. Height can be adjusted by judicious use of telephone directories etc.
Sit up straight, with a straight back, and without twisting the body. Always take care of your back muscles!

Good blood circulation

If brain and muscles are to cooperate optimally, it is vital to have good circulation. Just hold up one arm for a while, at the same time letting the other arm hang down. After a while compare the colour of the skin of either hand — and you'll see the difference between a good and a bad blood-supply! This will impress on you, too, the importance of sitting properly, of comfortable and roomy clothing, periods of relaxation etc. If your fingers get numb, this can be due to poor blood circulation, or to pressure on some nerve resulting from a wrong posture or nervous tension.

Relax!

You may find you're tense in your mouth, in your chin, feet, toes — yes, anywhere... If the body remains for long periods of time in a single fixed posture, the muscles can get tired, tense and tender. E.g. if your head is held rigid, you can get a stiff neck.
Relaxing the neck: make swaying movements with your head, easy and relaxed!
Relaxing the shoulders, arms, hands and fingers can be done as follows (among other ways):
Sit in the posture described above (see The Proper Way to Sit).
Let your arms hang loosely straight down until you almost feel them tugging at your shoulders.
Then gently move only your fingers.
Then slowly raise the forearms, using as little muscular strength as possible and without moving your shoulders.
Embrace the guitar. Let one arm at a time flop down, then, using as little muscular strength as possible, raise it to the playing position, the fingers lying loose on the strings. Pay attention to your shoulders, make no unnecessary movements, take the shortest way, adjust the position of the guitar until everything feels just as it ought to!
Play in short intense spurts. It's better to play for a quarter of an hour every day than for two hours once a week.
Take a hint from athletes. We musicians can learn a lot from their way of tackling problems of relaxation and physical fitness.

Relaxation

Stress and nervousness can be contributory causes of muscular tension. Before you start playing you should relax thoroughly for a little while from all your daily chores and worries. Before sitting down to play take a bath, drink a nice hot cup of tea. In a word, look after yourself and never let your ambitions rob you of the wonderful feeling of playfulness when "playing" a musical instrument.

MUSCULAR SENSE

When we talk about our "senses" we often tend to forget muscular sense. Its organs are scattered among the muscular fibres. Among other things they keep us informed of the muscles' state of tension. It seems that it is also in this way we get to know about the position of our limbs. Under normal conditions, for instance, we can put food to our mouth even in total darkness. It is with the aid of this sense that we estimate the weight of any object. If most of us can grab hold of an egg without crushing it it's because we can estimate the exact amount of muscular pressure needed. The javelin-thrower, the golfer etc. know all about this. And quite obviously we musicians too must learn to exploit our muscular sense to the utmost and not have to rely on the "controlling" action of the eye. Relatively speaking, the eye is a slow-witted instrument. (If you don't believe this, move your hand fast in front of your eye at a foot's distance and note what happens!)
Sit down at a table, reach out one arm to full length, and lay a finger on a definite spot on the table top. Now press it down repeatedly, firmly but lightly. *Remain as relaxed as possible* so that your muscular sense has every chance of establishing the arm's position and the exact spot where you have put your finger. Now take your hand away, relax, *close your eyes*, and replace your finger on the same spot. *You'll be astounded to see how close you've come to it. All this is also true of playing the guitar.*

Example: ①——**2**——7————

Put down your forefinger on fret 2 (see ex.), keep pressing lightly on the string; now glide to fret 7 (see ex.), and do the same. Now you've two spots between which you must try to glide to and from, swiftly and with your eyes closed. Then check up with eyes and ears. Finally with the ear alone.

Advice when playing chords

It is very common for players to get down-hearted or annoyed with their guitars when they can't get a chord "clean" — i.e., so that all its notes can be heard clearly, without any extraneous buzzings. But don't worry! Everything can be explained. For instance, turn to p. 28 and How You Avoid Buzzing. But here, too, you must exert just right amount of pressure. If you only press so loosely that the string buzzes, as so often happens, then it's not a bad idea to press a bit harder *on that string and no other*. Buzz comes from your failure to train the connections between your brain and each individual finger. Furthermore, strong pressure with one finger can counteract pressure from another. The following example shows why this is so:
Hold out your left hand straight in front of you, fingers outstretched. If you try to bend the third finger alone, the others will instinctively follow suit, unless you've more or less consciously switched on the muscular strength in the back of your hand, with orders to restrain these fingers. Until you've learnt just how much muscular strength you need, this restraining movement will tend to be exaggerated and excessive, *and this is another cause of muscular tension.*

Try this

To sum up: Here, as always, it's a question of remaining relaxed and using a minimum of movement and muscular strength.
Try out the A-major chord on the previous page: Place the fingers *lightly* on the strings. Press down *one string at a time* with a *swift* and *yielding* movement (i.e., immediately return to the relaxed position from which you started out, but without losing contact with the string). Then yield with *both* fingers at once in the same way, *simultaneously*. Then let your arm drop, so that your hand hangs down loosely. Close your eyes and try to bring into your mind's eye the image of the grip for A-major. Then concentrate mentally on the fingers which must make it, and where each finger must be placed. Then look and check where and how you have placed each finger.
Repeat the entire procedure from the beginning. This is a so-called "silent exercise", purely for the *left hand*.

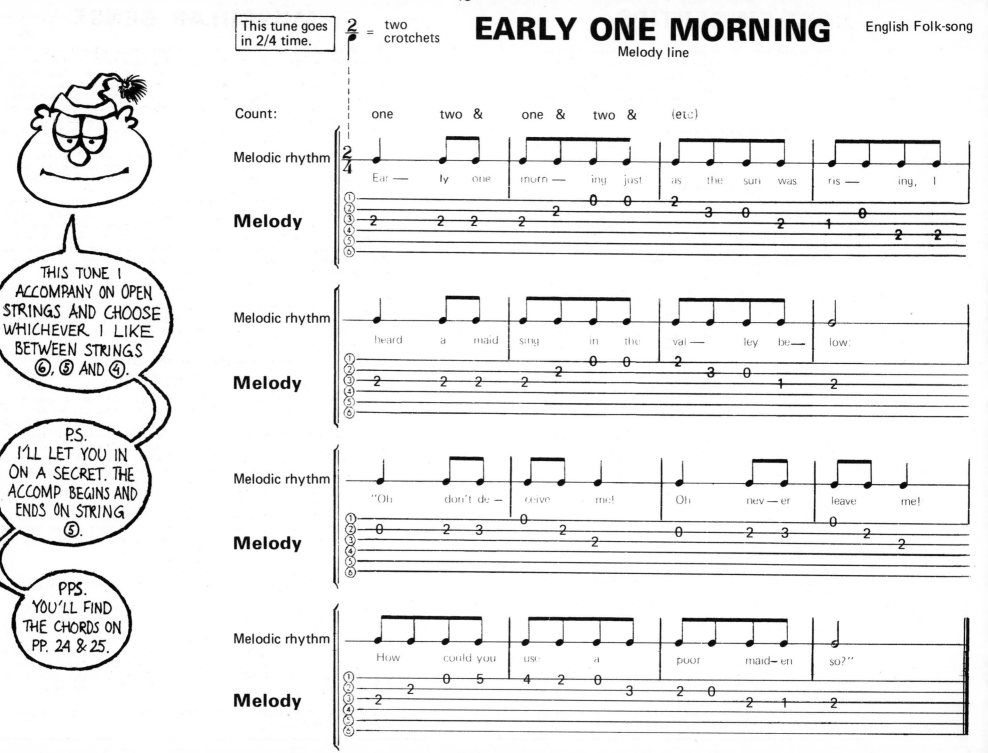

DOWN IN THE VALLEY

Melody line and accompaniment

Folk-song from the British Isles

THE TROLLS' LULLABY
Melody line and accompaniment

LEFT AND RIGHT HAND

Frets 10, 11, 12 etc are denoted by a l (without a serif) to avoid confusion with frets 1, 0, 1, 2 etc.

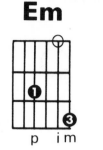
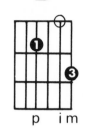
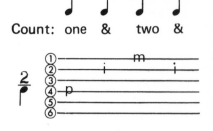

Em   **B**

Count: one & two &

Forefinger and third finger slip all the time up and down the strings as you shift between Em and B.

Make as little movements with the right-hand fingers as possible. Try to keep the tone pure!

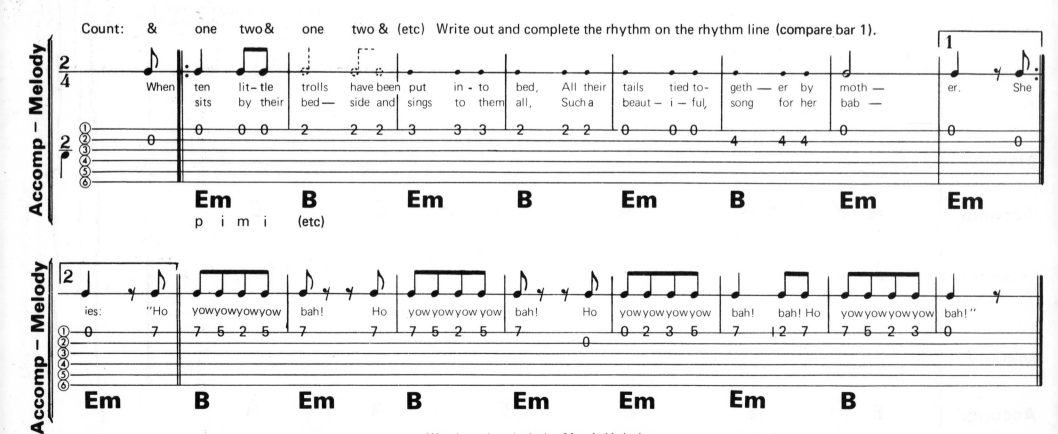

Words and melody by Margit Holmberg

ST. JAMES INFIRMARY BLUES
American Blues
Melody line and accompaniment

LEFT AND RIGHT HAND

Verse 1: It was down in old Joe's barroom,
On the corner by the square,
The drinks were served as usual,
And the usual crowd was there.

Verse 2: On my left stood Joe McKenney,
And his eyes were bloodshot red;
He turned to the crowd around him,
These are the words he said:

Verse 3: "As I passed by the old infirmary,
I saw my baby there;
She was lyin' on a long white table,
So sweet, so cool, so fair."

Verse 4: Oh, when I die, please bury me,
In my high-top Stetson hat;
Put a twenty-dollar gold piece on my watch chain,
So my friends'll know I died standin' pat.

Verse 5: Get six gamblers to carry my coffin,
Six chorus girls to sing me a song;
Put a jazz band on my tail gate,
To raise Hell as we go along.

Verse 6: "Now that's the end of my story;
Let's have another round of booze.
And if anyone should ask you, just tell them:
I've got the St. James Infirmary blues."

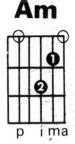
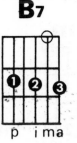

As you see, there are various types of chord having the same name. This is connected with your choice of tonal quality and playing technique.

LEFT AND RIGHT HAND

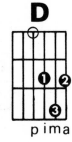

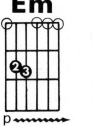

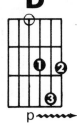

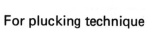

For plucking technique

For strumming technique

Hold the fingers of your left hand about 3—4 millimetres above the strings, in the shape of a D-major grip and thus ready to play, swiftly and simply, a D-major chord. Sometimes the third finger of the left hand tends involuntarily to act as a damper on string 1. For more about this, see p. 28 "How to Avoid Buzzing".

If, to begin with, the D-major chord gives you trouble, play D6 instead. This applies both to plucking and strumming.

D6

OH SINNERMAN

Accompaniment 2

This accompaniment is also intended for "What shall we do"

Accomp | **Em** / / / | **Em** / / / |

(Extra tune)

Oh,----- - sin —ner—man,------------where you gon—na-- run ------ to? ------
(What ----- shall--we--- do -------- with the ---- drunk—— en -------- sail ——— or?. . .)

Accomp | **D(6)** / / / | **D(6)** / / / |

Oh,------ - sin —ner—man-------------where you gon—na---run ------to? -------

Accomp | **Em** / / / | **Em** / / / |

Oh,------ - sin—ner—man,-------------- where you gon—na--- run ------ to,------

Accomp | **Em** / **D(6)** / | **Em** / / 𝄽 |

All --------------- on ------ that ----- day? ------------------

AS YOU CAN SEE, SHIPMATE, THERE'S TWO WAYS OF ACCOMPANYING. CHOOSE WHICH YOU LIKE BEST. — ME, I SWITCH FROM PLUCKING TO STRIKING THEM OL' STRINGS; AND TALKIN' O' DRUNKEN SAILORS, I USUALLY GIVEN 'EM THE SAME OLD CHORDS IN THE SAME OLD ORDER, YESSIR!

SKIP TO MY LOU
Accompaniment

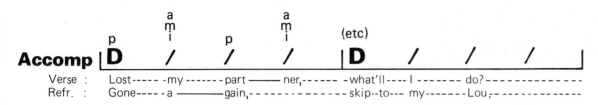

Accomp | D / / / | D / / / |
Verse : Lost ----- my ----- part —— ner, —— what'll ---- I ------ do? -------------
Refr. : Gone ---- a ——— gain, ------------- skip--to--- my ------ Lou, -----

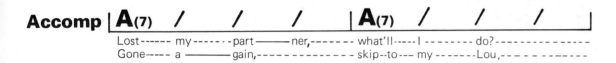

Accomp | A(7) / / / | A(7) / / / |
Lost ----- my ----- part —— ner, —— what'll ---- I ------ do? -------------
Gone ---- a ——— gain, ------------- skip--to--- my ------ Lou, -----

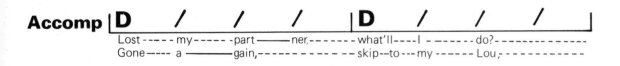

Accomp | D / / / | D / / / |
Lost ----- my ----- part —— ner, —— what'll ---- I ------ do? -------------
Gone ---- a ——— gain, ------------- skip--to--- my ------ Lou, -----

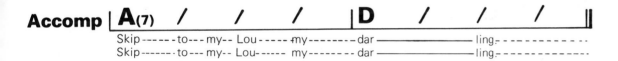

Accomp | A(7) / / / | D / / / ‖
Skip ----- to--- my-- Lou ----- my -------- dar ———————— ling. -----------
Skip ----- to--- my-- Lou ----- my -------- dar ———————— ling. -----------

Verse 2 : I'll get another one prettier than you, (3x)
          Skip to my Lou my darling.
Refr.   : Gone again, skip to my Lou, (3x)
          Skip to my Lou my darling.
Verse 3 : Little red wagon painted blue, (3x)
          Skip to my Lou my darling. (Refr.)

Verse 4 : Flies in the buttermilk two by two, (etc)

Verse 5 : Flies in the sugar bowl shoo shoo shoo, (etc)

Verse 6 : Going to Texas two by two, (etc)

Verse 7 : Cat's in the cream jar, what'll I do? (etc)

LEFT AND RIGHT HAND

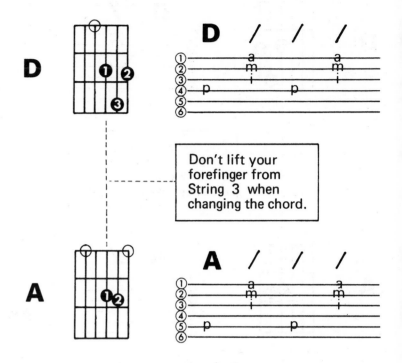

Don't lift your forefinger from String 3 when changing the chord.

Instead of the A-major chord you can play A-seventh = A7

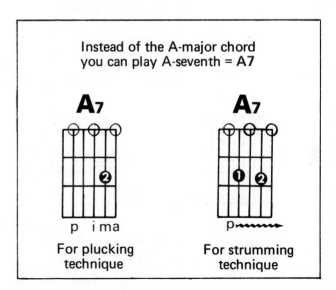

For plucking technique   For strumming technique

LEFT AND RIGHT HAND

D

D /

The forefinger must remain on the string at fret 2 when you move between D and A.

A

A /

The forefinger must slide on the string between fret 2 and 1 when you move between A and E.

E

E /

Instead of the E-major chord you can play E-seventh = E7 (see p. 44)

ON P. 17 UNDER THE HEADING "MUSCLE SENSE" IS SOME GOOD ADVICE FOR PLAYING CHORDS.

EARLY ONE MORNING
Accompaniment

Verse 1 :   Early one morning, just as the sun was rising, I heard a maid sing in the valley below:

Refr. :   "Oh, don't deceive me! Oh, never leave me! How could you use a poor maiden so?"

Verse 2 :   Oh, gay is the garland, and fresh are the roses, I've culled from the garden to bind on thy brow.

Refr. :   "Oh, don't deceive...

Verse 3 :   Remember the vows that you made to your Mary, Remember the bow'r where you vowed to be true.

Refr. :   "Oh, don't deceive...

Verse 4 :   Thus sang the poor maiden, her sorrows bewailing, Thus sang the poor maid in the valley below.

Refr. :   "Oh, don't deceive...

Accomp | A / | A / | D / | E / |

Ear — ly --- one --- morn — ing ··· just ---- as --- the-- sun ---was -----ris — ing,---I--

Accomp | A / | A / | D E | A / |

heard----- a -----maid---sing------ in --- the----- val —— ley--- be —— low:------------------

Accomp | E / | A / | E / | A / |

"Oh------- don't de —— ceive----- me! ------- Oh ----- nev—er ----leave---- me! -------

Accomp | A / | D / | A E | A / |

How------- could you ---- use ------ a ----------- poor ------maid—en ------so?"---------------

✶) To begin with, just play the bass with your thumb.

NOTE-FINDER

(over a C-major scale)

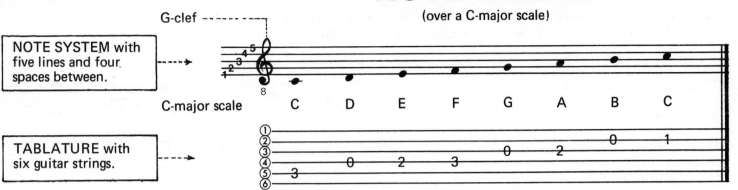

NOTE SYSTEM with five lines and four spaces between.

TABLATURE with six guitar strings.

An 8 under the G-clef = The guitar sounds an octave (8 notes) lower than written.

BASIC NOTES OF THE SCALE: C, D, E, F, G, A and B.

WCQFGZJ WCQFGZJ ZQWWZJ MWHP

Which melody line this is, you will find out if you translate the *notes below into tablature,* with the help of the *Note-finder.*

Note-finder

This Note-finder contains basic notes on all strings from the open string
up to fret 3, divided up into octaves. Each octave runs from C upwards to B.

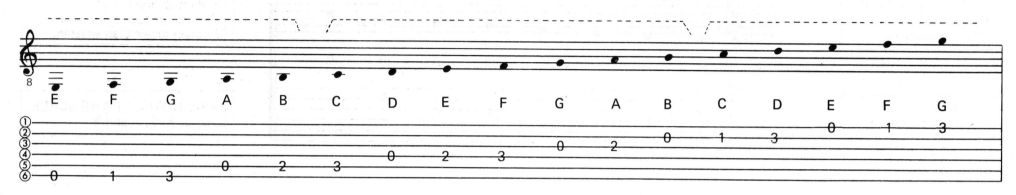

TASK 1: Translate the *notes* of the melody line
into tablature, with the help of
the *Note-finder* above.

JOHNNY'S SONG

Melody line and accompaniment

TASK 2: Translate other melodies that use only the
basic notes of the scale, using the Note-finder.
Music shops sell special Tablature paper.

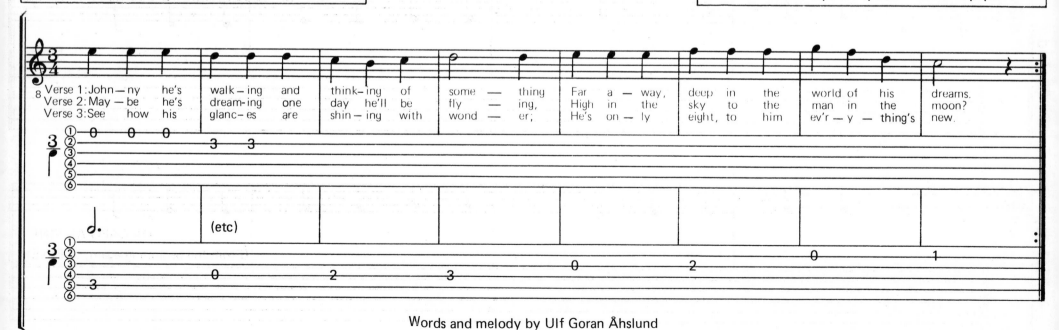

Words and melody by Ulf Goran Åhslund

THE DRAGON-FLY
Melody line and accompaniment

Gliding along the string
LEFT HAND
When you have to glide a finger between two frets on the same string, this is indicated by a dotted line on the tablature line: ----------------

See accompaniment below.

Verse 1: Dragonfly, dragonfly, why do you roam,
Hither and thither, say, have you no home?

Verse 2: "I fly about on this fine summer's day,
Peering and prying and looking each way."

Verse 3: Dragonfly, dragonfly, how can that be?
Tell me, how is it so much you can see?

Verse 4: "Oh it's so easy, if only you knew!
Two thousand eyes can see better than two!"

Alternating plucking fingers
RIGHT HAND
Try to switch fingers as you pluck the strings in the course of a tune.
E.g. m – i – m – i – m – i (etc)
E.g. a – i – a – i – a – i (etc)
E.g. a – m – a – m – a – m (etc)
E.g. a – m – i – a – m – i (etc)

TASK: Translate the *notes* of the melody line *into tablature,* with the help of the *Note-finder* on the previous page.

Words and melody by Lasse Sundberg

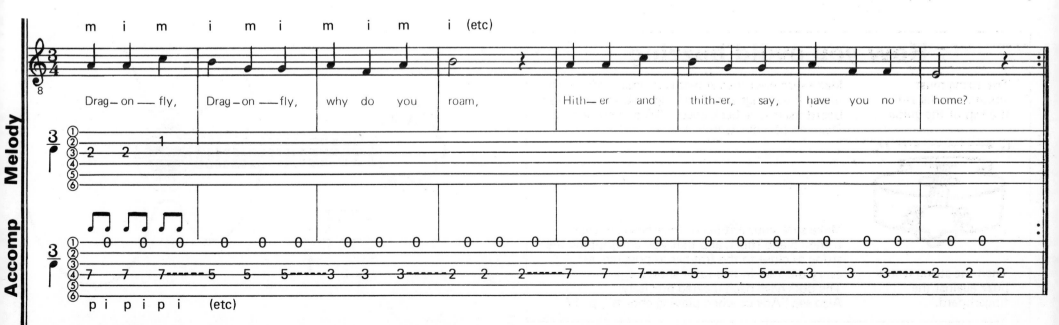

HOW YOU INFLUENCE THE CHARACTER, QUALITY AND STRENGTH OF THE TONE

How you pluck the string

BENDING STROKE

The finger *bends when plucking*, so that it *does not* touch the next string

STRAIGHT STROKE

The finger is held straight when plucking, so that it ends up on the next string

WITH FINGERNAILS

If you like you can play with the fingernails of your right hand. If so, they should project only 1 — 2 mm beyond your fingertips. You can also play with your fingertip and nail in the same stroke.

You can file your nails with a sandpaper file and polish them with the finest grade of emery cloth.

How you change tone-colour

You can change the *tone-colour* by plucking the string at *different points* between the bridge and the fingerboard.

3 important points of attack

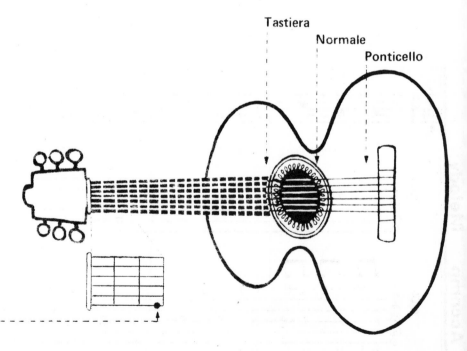

Tastiera

Normale

Ponticello

How you avoid buzzing

The string must vibrate parallel with the top of the guitar.

Then the string won't buzz against the fingerboard.

Make sure your instrument is in good order, particularly the strings and their height above the fingerboard itself (See back cover: "What You Should Demand of Your Guitar").

Make sure your left-hand fingernails are well-trimmed and short, and that you are gripping the string as close to the fret-bar as possible, as every diagram in this tutor shows, e.g.- - - - - The dots have been located precisely. Also see "Advice when playing chords", p. 17.

CLEMENTINE
Melody line and accompaniment

LEFT AND RIGHT HAND

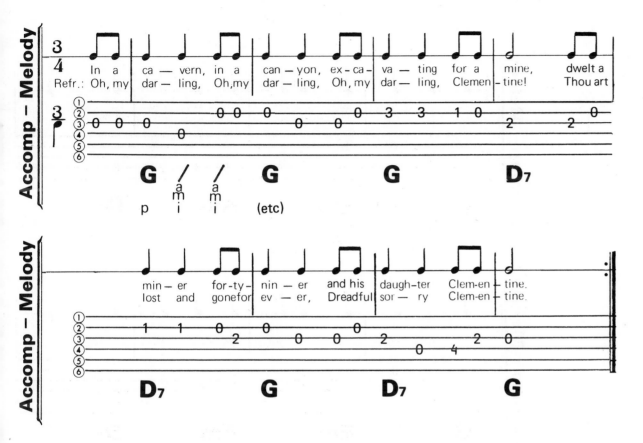

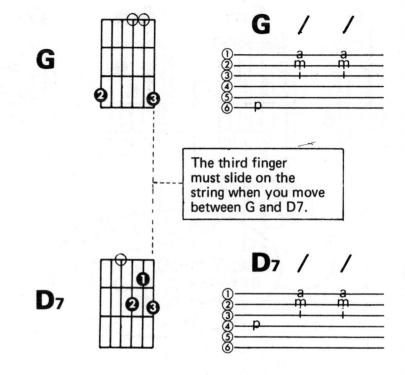

The third finger must slide on the string when you move between G and D7.

Verse 2 : Light she was and like a fairy,
and her shoes were number nine;
Herring-boxes, without topses,
sandals were for Clementine. (Refr.)

Verse 3 : Drove she ducklings to the water,
every morning just at nine,
Stubbed her toe upon a splinter,
fell into the foaming brine. (Refr.)

Verse 4 : Ruby lips above the water,
blowing bubbles soft and fine,
But alas I was no swimmer,
so I lost my Clementine. (Refr.)

Verse 5 : There's a churchyard, on the hillside,
where the flowers grow and twine,
There grow roses, mongst the posies,
fertilized by Clementine. (Refr.)

Verse 6 : In my dreams she still doth haunt me,
robed in garments soaked in brine;
Though in life I used to hug her,
now she's dead I'll draw the line. (Refr.)

Verse 7 : How I missed her, how I missed her,
how I missed my Clementine!
But I kissed her little sister,
and forgot my Clementine. (Refr.)

An old nugget re-discovered in the 1849 Gold Rush

Below, you will find two more types of right-hand action for sounding the strings, written out for a G-major chord. Vary the D7-chord in the same way!

LEFT AND RIGHT HAND

G   **Em**   **Am**   **D₇**

p i m a   p i m a   p i m a   p i m a

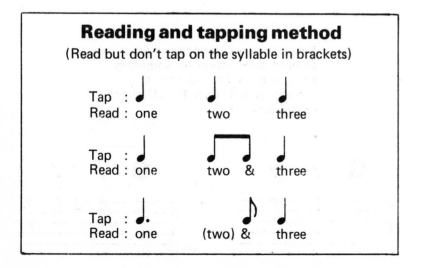

THESE CHORDS WILL DO NICELY FOR MOLLY MALONE, TRY TO REMEMBER, AULD LANG SYNE AND OTHER TUNES TOO.

♩. = dotted crotchet

Reading and tapping method
(Read but don't tap on the syllable in brackets)

Tap : ♩   ♩   ♩
Read : one   two   three

Tap : ♩   ♩ ♩   ♩
Read : one   two & three

Tap : ♩.   ♪   ♩
Read : one   (two) & three

BEYOND THE TWILIGHT
Melody line and accompaniment

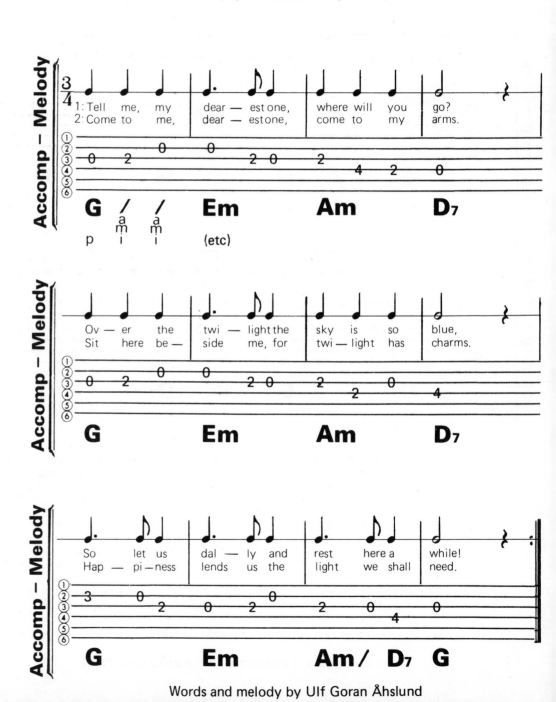

Words and melody by Ulf Goran Åhslund

DARK EYES
Melody line and accompaniment

LEFT AND RIGHT HAND

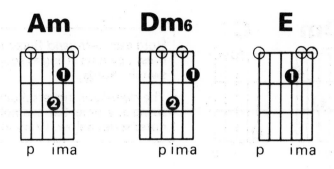

Russian Folk-tune

LEFT AND RIGHT HAND

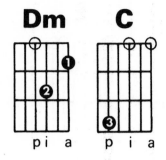

Dm   **C**

Hold each *left-hand* finger ready to press down its string as soon as you switch chords.

The *right-hand* fingers pluck one string at a time. See example of notes series below. (Vary at will!)

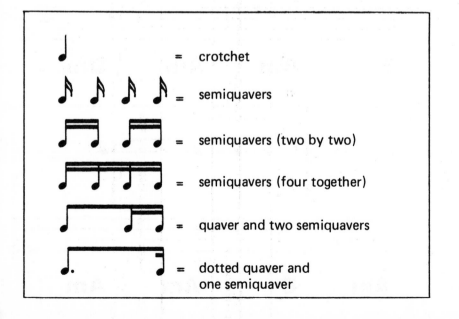

- ♩ = crotchet
- = semiquavers
- = semiquavers (two by two)
- = semiquavers (four together)
- = quaver and two semiquavers
- = dotted quaver and one semiquaver

WHAT SHALL WE DO

Melody line and accompaniment 3

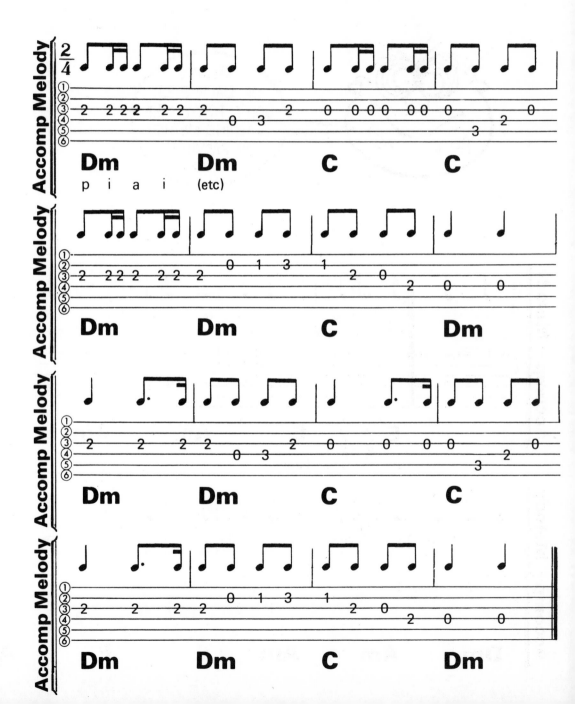

VARIOUS WAYS OF PLAYING C AND G7-CHORDS

Chords marked C are based on the note C, those marked G7 are based on the note G, etc. But if you want to play another bass note, then this is indicated by a little letter after a stroke.
Below you can see four combinations with varying uses of C and G7, and how they are notated. The diagram can also serve as an example of technical simplification.

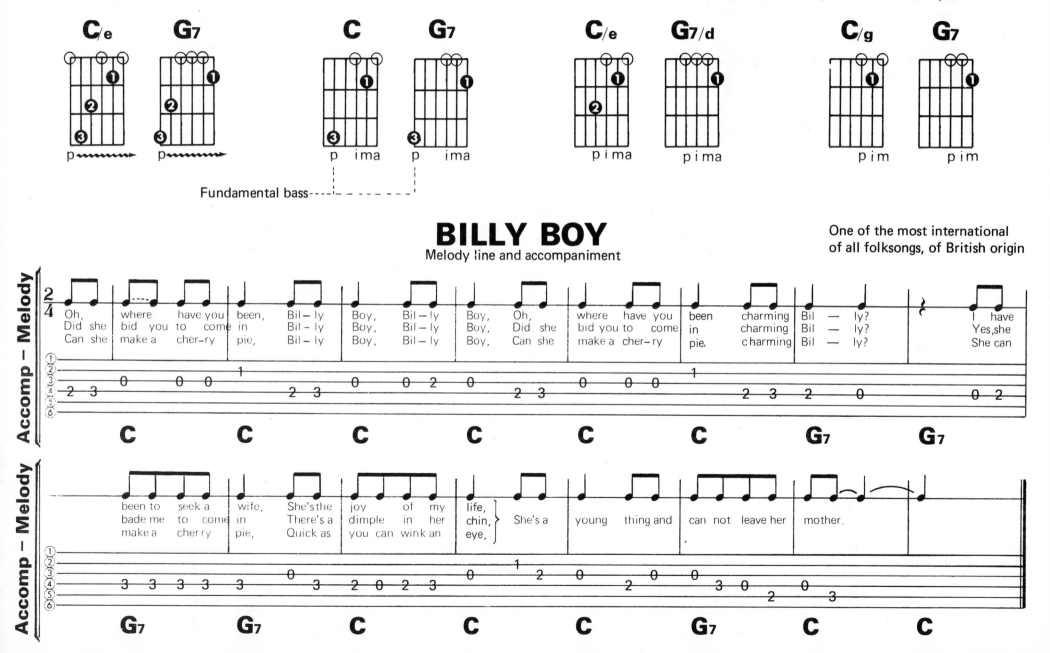

BILLY BOY
Melody line and accompaniment

One of the most international of all folksongs, of British origin

SHARPS, FLATS & NATURALS

Notes with sharps or flats in front of them are called "accidentals" (as are the sharp and flat signs themselves)

Sharp

raise the note by a semitone (= one fret *upwards* on the guitar).
The note is then called e.g. C-sharp, D-sharp etc.

Flat

lower the note by a semitone (= one fret *downwards* on the guitar).
Then the note is called e.g. D-flat, E-flat etc.

Natural

cancel out a sharp or flat.

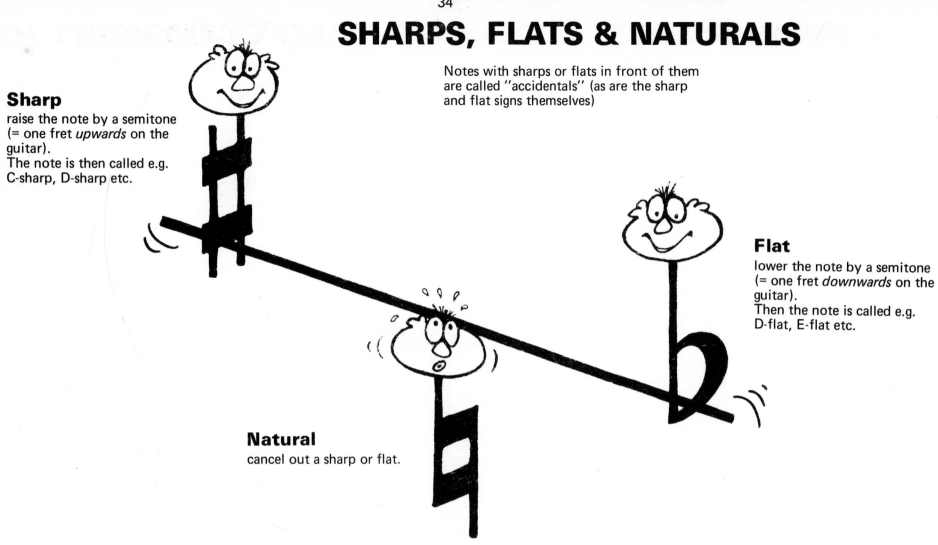

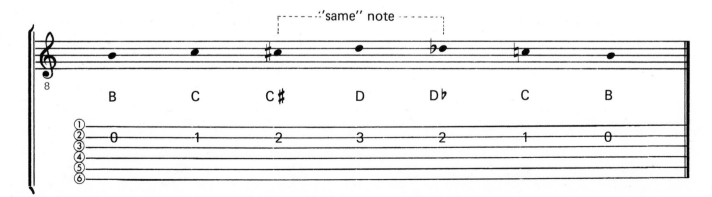

G-MAJOR SCALE
The note F raised F sharp

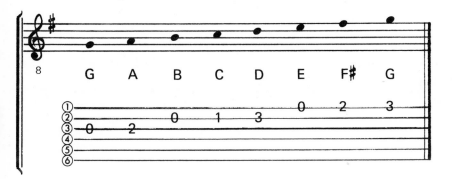

LEFT AND RIGHT HAND

G
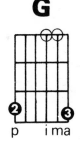
p i ma

C
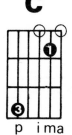
p i ma

D7
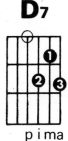
p i ma

Fixed Key-signatures

apply throughout a whole piece, except where a change is indicated. You'll find the key-signature (sharps and flats) immediately to the right of the clef sign.
E.g.

Orchestra

Here are two kinds of accomp: Chords and accomp line. Several guitars together can add up to an orchestra! The accomp line (here a pure G-major scale) can equally be played by some other instrument, e.g. a recorder.

All the world's birthday song

HAPPY BIRTHDAY
Melody line and accompaniment

Words and music by Mildred and Patty S. Hill

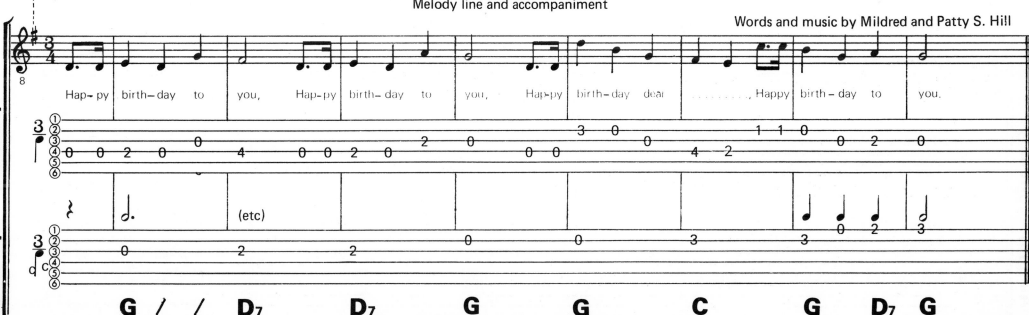

JOSEPHINA BLUES
Melody line and accompaniment

Words and melody by Ulf Goran Åhslund

Fixed Key-signature   Accidental sharp   Accidental flat

Jo — se — phine, oh   Jo — se — phine, oh   sit you down and play me a blues.

FINE

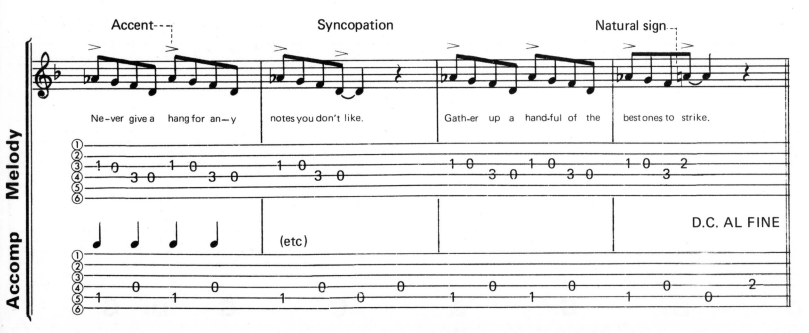

Accent - - -   Syncopation   Natural sign - - -

Ne-ver give a hang for an—y   notes you don't like.   Gath-er up a hand-ful of the   best ones to strike.

D.C. AL FINE

Accidental sharps and flats

apply only within the bar where they appear.

Alla breve

which is sometimes written ₵ means that the piece goes to a two-in-a-bar beat, which makes for a brisker rhythm.

Accents

show which notes should be emphasized. They are written either above or below the note.

Syncopation

means a deviation from the normal emphasis on the notes.

Normal emphasis in 4/4 time:

Example of syncopated 4/4 time:

Improvisation

is a characteristic of blues and jazz, so by all means change both rhythm and melody here and there, if you feel that way. For more about blues, see p. 42.

MOLLY MALONE
Melody line and accompaniment

LEFT AND RIGHT HAND

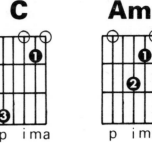
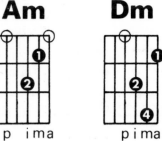
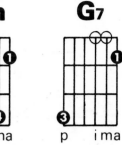

Irish Folksong

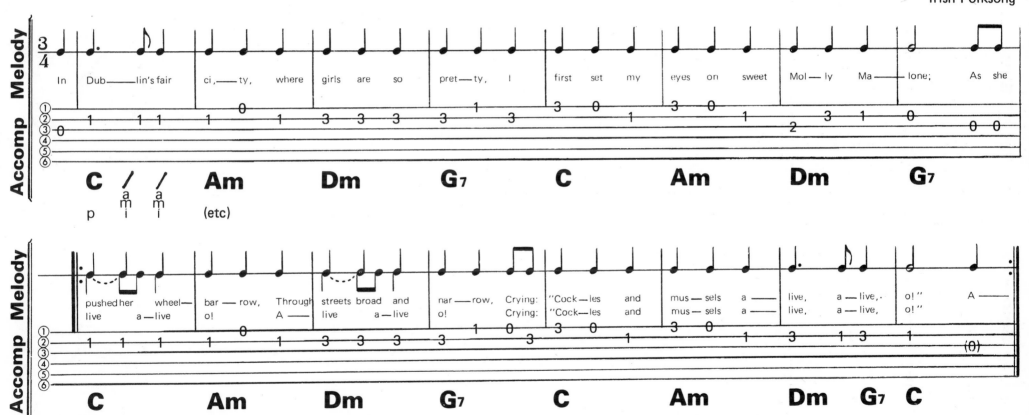

Verse 2: She was a fishmonger, but sure 'twas no wonder,
For so were her father and mother before;
And they each pushed their wheel-barrow,
Throught streets broad and narrow,
Crying: "Cockles and mussels alive, alive-o!" (Refr.)

Verse 3: She died of a "faver", and no one could save her,
And that was the end of sweet Molly Malone;
But her ghost wheels her barrow,
Through streets broad and narrow,
Crying: "Cockles and mussels alive, alive-o!" (Refr.)

MALAGUEÑA
Solo

A Malagueña is a Spanish dance much like a fandango, from the province of Malaga; also a song, often sung in a more or less improvised fashion over a characteristic and recurrent progression of harmonies = E — Am —G —F — E.

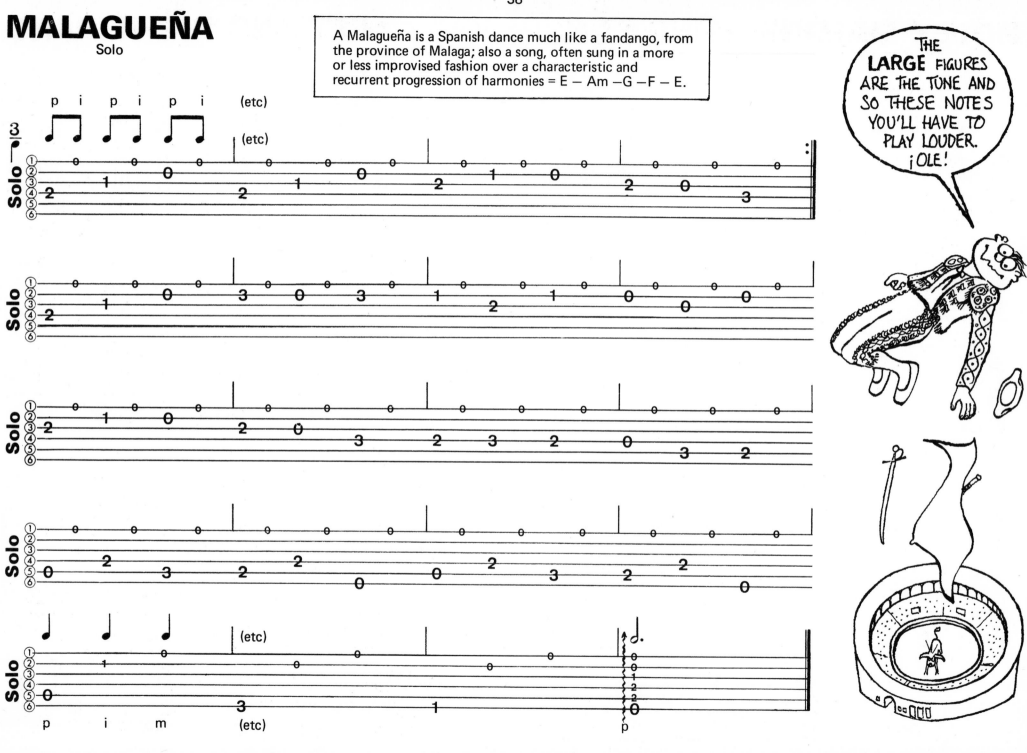

HOUSE OF THE RISING SUN

Melody line and accompaniment

American Blues from New Orleans

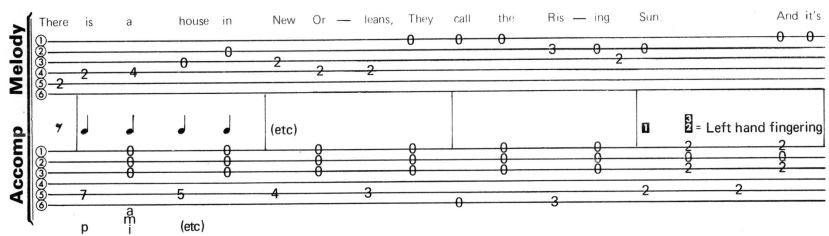

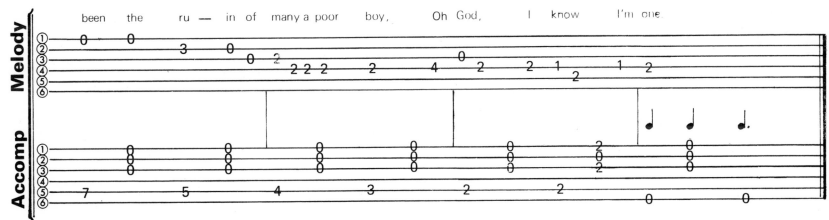

Verse 2: My mother was a tailor,
Sewed my new blue jeans.
My father was a gamblin' man
Down in New Orleans.

Verse 3: Now the only thing a gambler needs
Is a suitcase and a trunk.
And the only time he'll be satisfied
Is when he's all all adrunk.

Verse 4: Oh! mother, tell your children,
Not to do what I have done.
Spend your lives in sin and misery
In the House of the Rising Sun.

Verse 5: Well, I've got one foot on the platform,
The other foot on the train.
I'm going back to New Orleans
To wear that ball and chain.

Left-hand fingering for tablature

In connection with *tablature* the *left-hand* fingering is placed above the accomp line.

Barré

When using a barré, one finger grips across two or more strings.

Barré over three strings with forefinger.

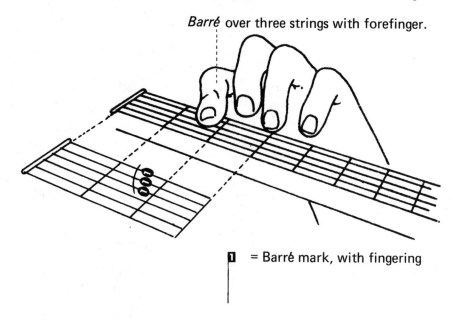

1 = Barré mark, with fingering

Note-finder

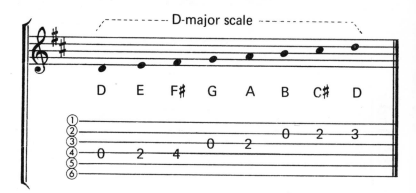

TASK: Translate the *written notes* of the melody line into *tablature* using the above.

THE MAID BY THE WELL
Melody line and accompaniment

Folk-song from Bohuslän, Sweden

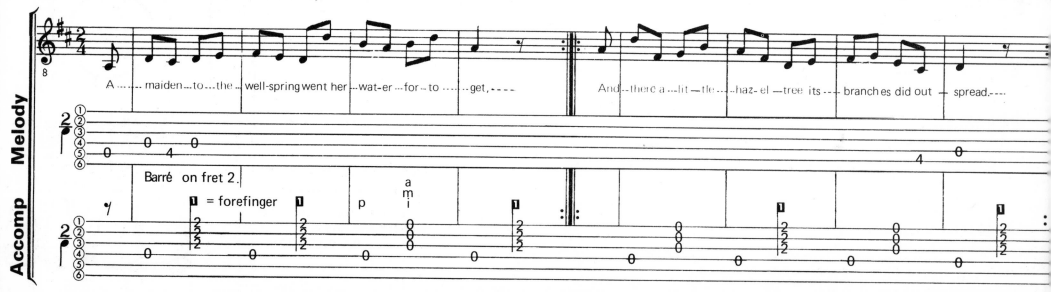

MICHAEL, ROW THE BOAT ASHORE

Melody line and accompaniment

Verse 1: Michael, row the boat ashore,
Alleluya! (2x)

Verse 2: Michael's boat is a music boat,
Alleluya! (2x)

Verse 3: Sister help to trim the sail,
Alleluya! (2x)

Verse 4: Jordan's river is chilly and col',
Alleluya!
Kills the body but not the soul,
Alleluya!

Verse 5: Jordan's river is deep and wide,
Alleluya!
Meet my mother on the other side,
Alleluya!

American Gospel

Extra task

If you like, you can translate the tablature into ordinary notation with the aid of the Note-finder on the previous page. Use ordinary music paper.

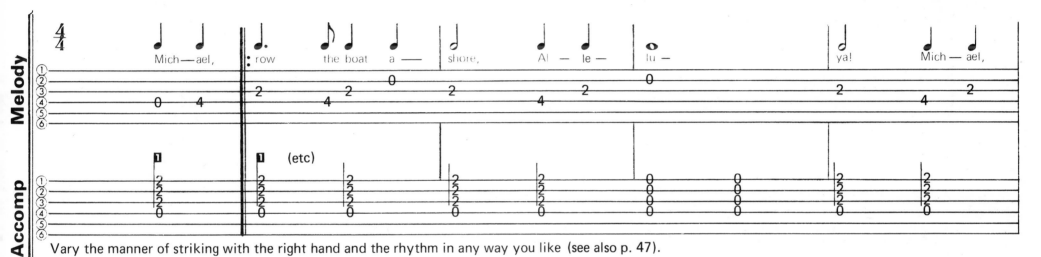

Vary the manner of striking with the right hand and the rhythm in any way you like (see also p. 47).

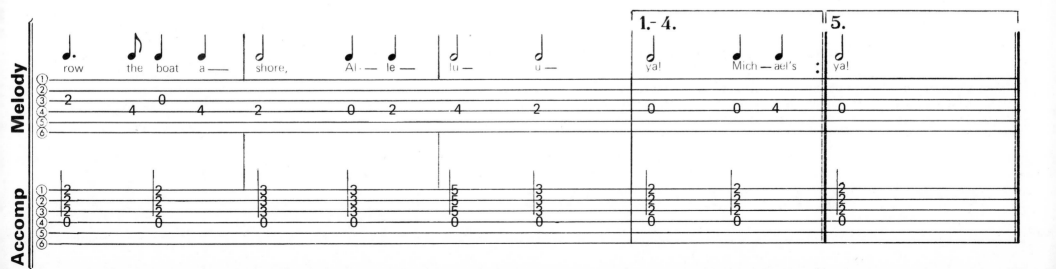

BLUES

The term "blues" comes from the "blue notes" — notes specially coloured by modifying their pitch slightly so that it becomes wavering and uncertain. This applies especially to the third note of the scale, which, e.g. in C-major, becomes a sort of mongrel note somewhere between E and E flat (E♭). See following example:

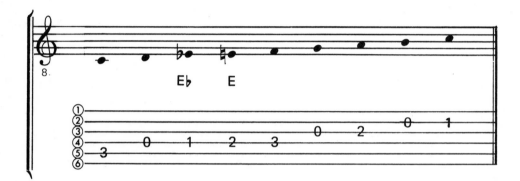

Singers can easily vary the pitch of a note to make it blue. A guitarist does so by stretching his string, and a pianist by striking two neighbouring notes at the same time, or almost. Listen to some blues guitarist, e.g., one of Josh White's or Leadbelly's recordings, to the blues singer Bessie Smith or the blues pianists Pete Johnson, Albert Ammons, etc, and note how they get their blues effects!

Blues – a means of expression

Blues are above all a means of expressing strong feeling and can therefore be executed differently in different contexts (Cf. the blues melodies in this tutor). But there are also generally recognized standard forms for their harmonic progressions and the number of bars involved. A very common type is the 12-bar kind you can see below and on the next page.

‖ C | ⁄ | ⁄ | C₇ | F₇ | ⁄ | C | ⁄ | F₇ | G₇ | C | ⁄ ‖

LEFT AND RIGHT HAND

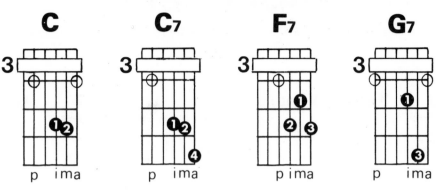

Choose whatever rhythm and type of plucking technique you like.

Alternative chords

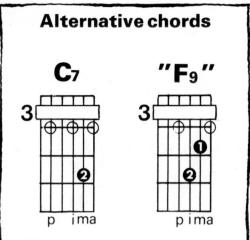

The chord in inverted commas is incomplete as F9, but still sounds nice in the context.

BLUES IN MY MIND

Melody line and accompaniment

Examples of blue note effects in this piece are marked by brackets.

Melody by Ulf Goran Åhslund

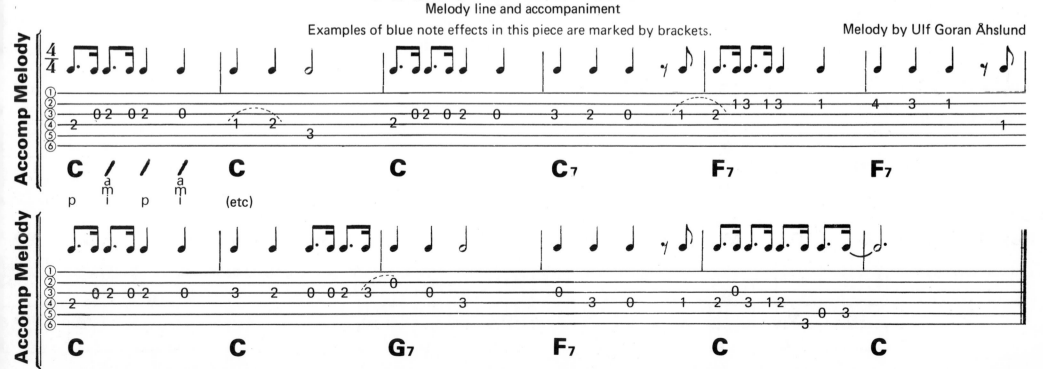

CHANGE OF KEY USING A CAPOTASTO
MAJOR KEYS

On these two pages you'll find "stacks" of keys which can be played with one and the same fingerings using a capotasto.

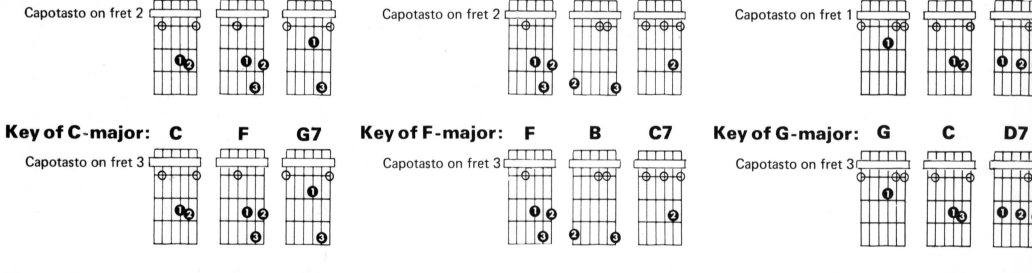

Key of A-major: A D E7 — Without capotasto

Key of D-major: D G A7 — Without capotasto

Key of E-major: E A B7 — Without capotasto

Key of B-major: B E F♯7 — Capotasto on fret 2

Key of E-major: E A B7 — Capotasto on fret 2

Key of F-major: F B♭ C7 — Capotasto on fret 1

Key of C-major: C F G7 — Capotasto on fret 3

Key of F-major: F B C7 — Capotasto on fret 3

Key of G-major: G C D7 — Capotasto on fret 3

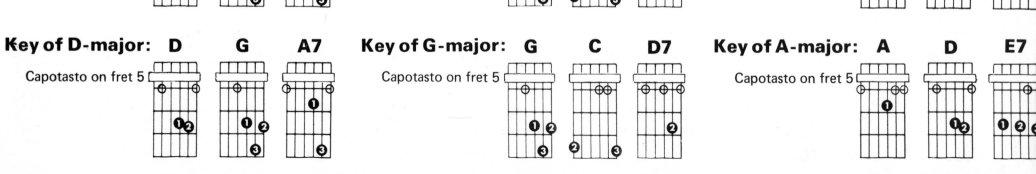

Key of D-major: D G A7 — Capotasto on fret 5

Key of G-major: G C D7 — Capotasto on fret 5

Key of A-major: A D E7 — Capotasto on fret 5

CHANGE OF KEY USING A CAPOTASTO
MINOR KEYS

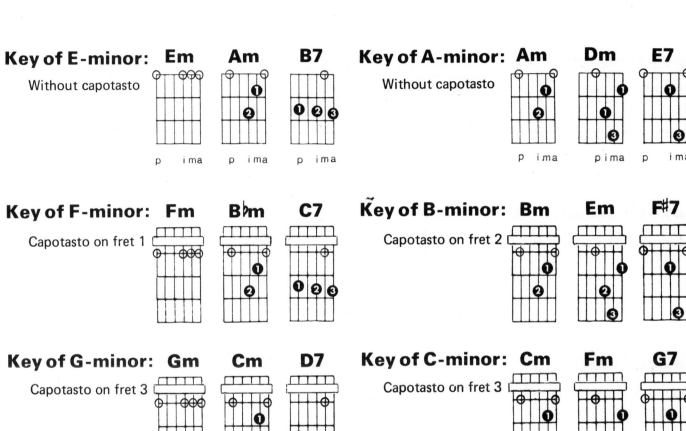

Key of E-minor: Em   Am   B7
Without capotasto

Key of A-minor: Am   Dm   E7
Without capotasto

Key of F-minor: Fm   B♭m   C7
Capotasto on fret 1

Key of B-minor: Bm   Em   F♯7
Capotasto on fret 2

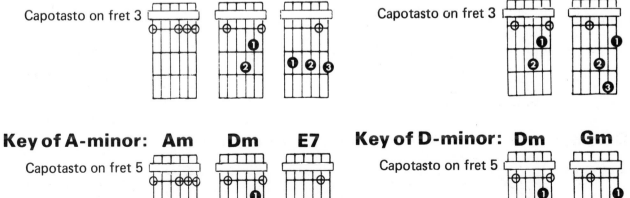

Key of G-minor: Gm   Cm   D7
Capotasto on fret 3

Key of C-minor: Cm   Fm   G7
Capotasto on fret 3

Key of A-minor: Am   Dm   E7
Capotasto on fret 5

Key of D-minor: Dm   Gm   A7
Capotasto on fret 5

THE COMMONEST CHORDS IN FOUR MAJOR KEYS
USING A CAPOTASTO AND THE SAME GRIP

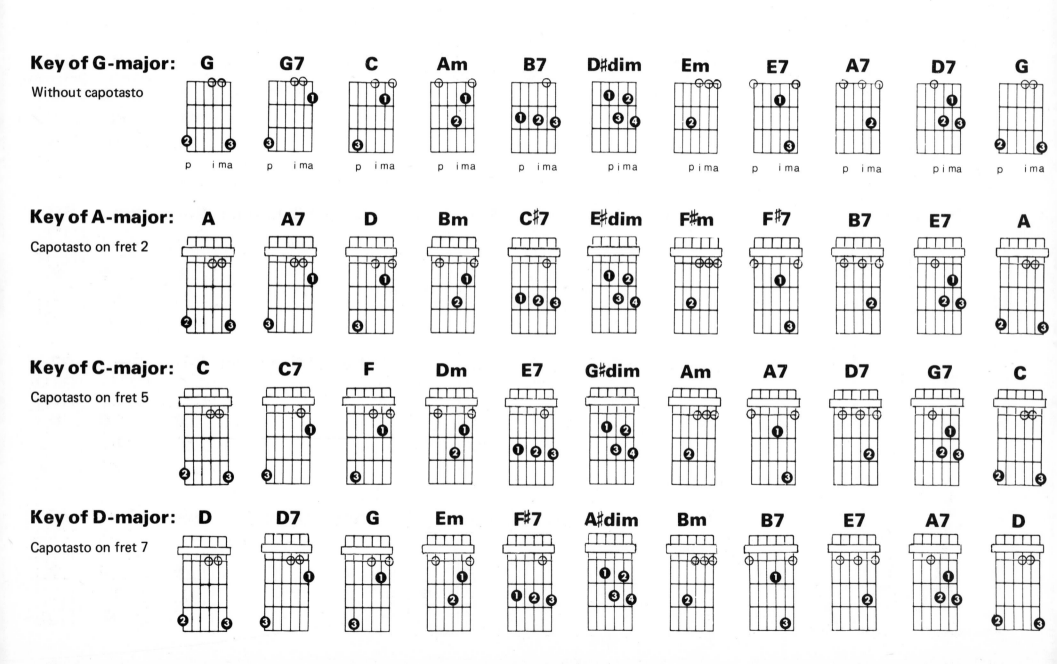

SOME COMMON RHYTHMS

Play the rhythms below on open strings and then on various chords or sequences of chords.
Bear in mind that there are many ways of playing rhythms: these are only a few examples.

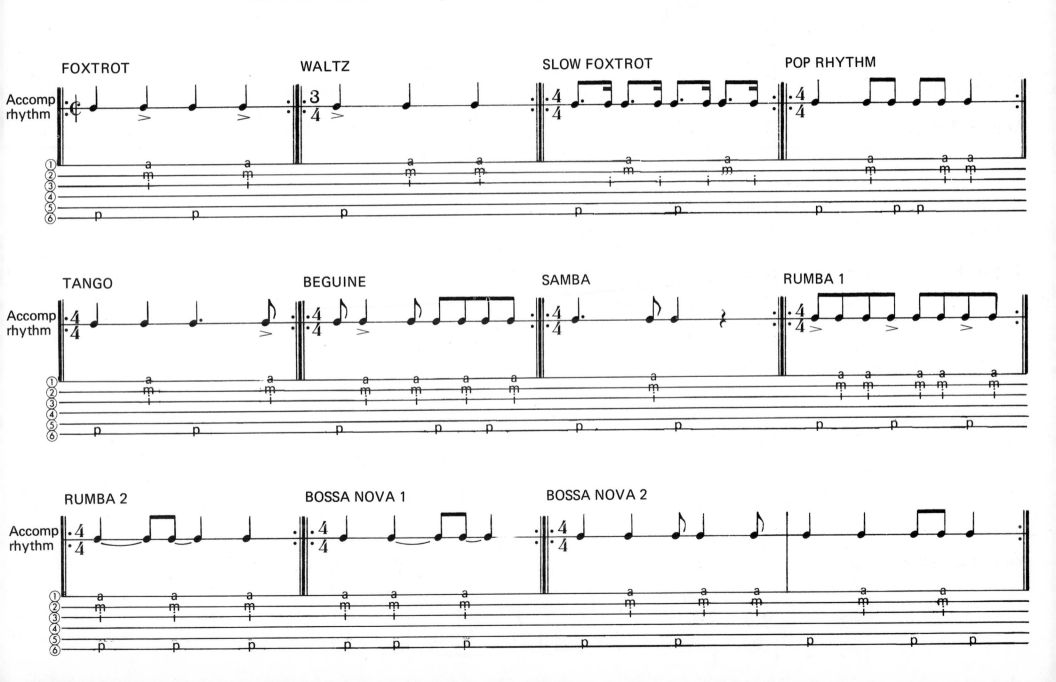

CHORDS! CHORDS! CHORDS! LOTS OF CHORDS!

Dear you!

So that's it! Now we've got to the last page and it's swarming all over with keys and chords. We just take our pick! Whether to pluck or strum the strings - it's all up to us now. Though of course we mustn't forget to think which strings are allowed into the chord. If you strum across the strings, then you must dampen strings marked "x" (See Gm).

And that's just about all there is to it, so far. So get going with the next book, e.g. Part 2 of this tutor! Coming with us?

Yours now and forever

Floppy